Charles Garnier's Opéra

Text
Gérard **Fontaine**

Photographs
Jean-Pierre **Delagarde**

ÉDITIONS DU PATRIMOINE
CENTRE DES
MONUMENTS NATIONAUX

Let's have a look at a few of the major dates in the history of the Palais Garnier.

5 January 1875

Marshal Mac-Mahon, president of the French Republic, accompanied by his wife, the duchess of Magenta, inaugurated the new Paris opera house in the presence of the king of Spain, the Lord Mayor of London, and two thousand personalities who had come from all over Europe.

That evening, the new building was indisputably the main event. In the press's view, the evening was first and foremost the triumph of the monument and of its architect, Charles Garnier. Garnier, who had not been invited, had to pay for his box in the upper circle—120 francs (over 1,000 euros)—an example of the government's thoughtfulness.

The president of France was there, of course, as was the young king of Spain, Alfonso XII, accompanied by his mother, Queen Isabella II; the Lord Mayor of London was there, of course, as were his sheriffs, heralds, and mace bearers; all the illustrious figures of Paris and elsewhere had, of course, pulled strings to be there. There was also a show on stage—a pretty poor one was the general opinion, a selection of successful operas and ballets of the period.

The main façade of the Palais Garnier illuminated at night. Chandeliers twinkle in the windows of the grand foyer.

Introduction

During the interval, there was a revolution in the mores of high society, a reflection of the public's fascination for the building. Until then, high-society ladies received visitors in their boxes; it would have been inconceivable for them to leave them to go for a walk in the foyers. Yet in Paris, on 5 January 1875, led by the queen of Spain on the arm of her royal son, the ladies, followed by their escorts and surrounded by a crowd of onlookers, did just that. Henceforth, with or without the pretext of admiring Paul Baudry's paintings, ladies wanted to escape during the intervals—a new stage in their ongoing liberation. And, at the end of the performance, the crowd going down the grand staircase cheered Charles Garnier. In late January 1875, Albert de Lasalle summed it up in a few lines in *Le Monde illustré*: "Nonetheless, it was many months before the Opéra became the premier opera house in France and more than just an architectural event. The frame has eclipsed the painting. To date, at least,

The Cortège of the Lord Mayor of London in the Grand Staircase on the Evening of the Inauguration of the Palais Garnier, 5 January 1875 by Édouard Detaille. Drawing heightened with gouache, commissioned by the French state on 9 January 1875 (Musées des Châteaux de Versailles et de Trianon, Versailles). A great spectacle, like that Garnier dreamed of for his grand staircase-theatre. Detaille presciently depicted the architect as the master of the house welcoming the Lord Mayor, while the head of state, Marshal Mac-Mahon, was a mere spectator; the director of the Opéra, Olivier Halanzier, is just a face in the crowd. Poetic truth takes precedence over protocol and historical accuracy.

the performances at the Opéra do not seem to have been an absolute necessity since it is the Opéra itself that people come to see." A case that is unique in the history of the building, for months after the inauguration, bookings were made without advance knowledge of what work was going to be performed or of the cast. Everything sold out, and Olivier Halanzier, the director, did not have to make much of an effort. Moreover, as soon as the opera house opened, to swell its already tidy accounts, he had introduced visits of the building during the day; the price was high—2.50 francs per person (25 euros)— but these visits, too, were always sold out. So, yes, the frame had eclipsed the painting. An observation that is still valid a century later. In the 1960s, during the difficult period that preceded the arrival of Rolf Liebermann, the Palais Garnier was still sold out—or mostly filled—every evening. In 1963 the average attendance was 70 per cent; the monument itself was a show that was worth the trip, whether the performance was good or bad. It was very difficult to get seats after the Opéra de Paris became one of the leading operas in the world under the management of Liebermann, from 1973 to 1980.

This fact was enthusiastically recognised by the public, but it did not go without saying. The construction of the building was marked by scandals—the attack on *The Dance* by Jean-Baptiste Carpeaux was the most memorable, but it was not the only one; the paintings by Gustave Boulanger in the Foyer de la Danse and even the innocent lamppost statues by Félix Chabaud, the charming *Morning Star* and *Evening Star* that illuminate the exterior balustrades, provoked the prudes of Paris; throughout the construction of the building, the court (in its own time), the Chamber, and the city council resounded with their protests.

Artistic controversies also raged; commentators found the polychromy of the building surprising. Garnier later retorted: "I imagined that a theatre should look cheerier than a prison, as a woman at a ball should look smarter than a slattern doing the washing-up" (Charles Garnier, *Le Nouvel Opéra de Paris*, vol. I [Paris: Ducher, 1878], 22). Of course, there were howls of indignation about the cost, an old tradition in a country that has never wanted to admit that what is most essential is the non-essential, that the non-essential is priceless, whether the ministry eggheads like it or not. Well, it is the non-essential that peoples identify with and in which they invest their imagination. What could be more superfluous than a cathedral, the Château de Versailles, or the Eiffel Tower? It is, nevertheless, from these non-essentials that the French get a sense of pride; it is thanks to non-essentials that other countries acknowledge them, respect them.

Nevertheless, Garnier worked wonders to make economies. For example, he considerably reduced his planned programme of gilding. Originally, all the decorative motifs of the rooftops were supposed to be gilded and linked to the groups of the façade and the lyre of Apollo at the top of the gable wall and the large ribs of the three domes—that of the auditorium and those of the east and west pavilions. The Kremlin, more or less. Already, in 1867, when the façades were unveiled for the Universal Exposition, their gilding had set some teeth on edge. After the Franco-Prussian War of 1870, when construction started again, Garnier, of course, wanted to finish the gilding that was underway when war broke out, particularly the gilt decorations of the central dome. When the public noticed the gilding, there was a general outcry. While 5 billion gold francs had to be raised to liberate the country, the architect, as reckless as he was extravagant, dared to spread them all over the roof of his monument. Garnier quickly had to cover the impudent gilt decorations with bronze-coloured paint. Only the parts gilded before the war remained gilded, and no more gilding was carried out.

In actual fact, the undertaking suffered throughout construction as a result of an initial misunderstanding: to have the project passed, the imperial government had cheated over its cost. In his preliminary studies, in 1861, Garnier had estimated the cost at 29 million gold francs. In the face of the entreaties of the minister in charge, he had to reduce it to 24 million gold francs, then to 18 million gold francs. And the Conseil des Bâtiments Civils imposed a limit of 15 million gold francs. There was no getting away from the facts—when the architect redid all his calculations in 1864, he again arrived at the figure of 21 million gold francs because of, in particular, the "surprises"

of the plot. Chosen without Garnier having been consulted, the plot was located on a water table that, even after having been pumped for several months, meant that an immense leakproof tank had to be built. It inspired the idea of the underground palace and lake of Gaston Leroux's *Le Fantôme de l'Opéra* (*The Phantom of the Opera*), but swallowed up Garnier's budget.

All told, the new Opéra cost 36 million gold francs (329 million euros). By way of comparison, Les Halles in Paris, built by Victor Baltard from 1851 to 1874, cost 50 million gold francs. But only the imagination counts. The Palais Garnier looks costly, even though its marble was barely more expensive than freestone. It was common knowledge that its architect was a spendthrift who wanted to adorn his monument with all the treasures of Golconda. During the inauguration, the press did not stop talking about the luxuriousness of the monument. In *Le Monde illustré* of 9 January 1875, Albert de Lasalle wrote of a "mountain of marble, porphyry, and bronze", of a "monolith like those erected by the Egyptians in times of legend". He was delighted because "the good, beautiful, and substantial millions of our country performed the miracle of making habitable this imposing and sumptuous accumulation of expensive stones". He was the only one.

The worst almost happened soon after the defeat of 1870. Many voices were raised to call for a halt to the construction, or even the demolition of the failed survivor of imperial pomp. Might this have been the cause of the relative rejection of the monument in certain circles? Did it seem, does it seem, today still, too closely linked to the Second Empire, whose errors the French collective imagination has not yet forgiven? In fact, the new Opéra ties to the imperial government were not as close as usually thought; the imperial government above all implemented a project that should have been launched long ago, supported it half-heartedly, and did not have the time to finish it.

Let's go back seventeen years.

Harmony by Charles Gumery. Gilt electroplated bronze, 1869. In the background, the silhouette of *Apollo, Poetry, and Music* by Aimé Millet—at the top of the stage wall pediment—stands out against the twilight. From the lyre of Apollo to the groups of the façade, gold was supposed to have glittered all over the domes and rooftops; the difficult times did not allow it, but Gumery's groups, executed before the fall of the empire and recently restored, bear witness to Garnier's programme.

14 January 1858

Their Majesties the Emperor and the Empress miraculously escaped a horrible assassination attempt by Italian anarchists with bombs when they were on their way the Opéra. There were several deaths and many injured.

As Napoleon III and Empress Eugénie's carriage, surrounded by a crowd of spectators and onlookers, drew up in front of the opera house then located on the Rue Le Peletier (its entrance was near the present no. 14), Italian plotters led by Felipe Orsini hurled three bombs that missed the imperial couple but killed eight people and wounded one hundred and fifty.

This assassination attempt prompted Napoleon III to intervene militarily to liberate Italy from Austria. It also meant that a new theatre, which would replace that of the Rue Le Peletier, had to be built. The Le Peletier opera house had been built by the architect François Debret to replace temporarily the Salle Montansier, demolished in 1820 on the orders of Louis XVIII after the assassination of the Duc de Berry. The Salle Le Peletier was inaugurated the following year, on 16 April 1821. In 1858 the dangers of the "temporary" location of nearly forty years had been revealed by Orsini's assassination attempt. It was finally decided to build an opera house worthy of the French capital.

These dramatic beginnings explain the importance accorded to the service of the emperor: Garnier had planned to allocate the entire west pavilion to him. Accessible via a wide ramp, the pavilion was meant to allow the sovereigns to get out of their carriage far from the rest of the audience, enter a circular interior hall, and to head directly to their box. Complemented by salons, the space would have looked grand and allowed the head of state to feel safe in a setting in keeping with his rank. After the fall of the empire in 1870, the execution of this part of the programme was suspended. Garnier was unable to prevent all the spaces reserved for the head of state from being transformed into a library and museum; he even had to carry out the conversion.

But let's get back to the history of the construction of the Nouvel Opéra (its official name at the time).

30 May 1861

A young unknown architect wins the competition for the new opera house.

Instituted by the decree of 29 December 1860, the competition for the construction of a new opera house gave candidates a month to submit a preliminary design. This was a first. At the time, architects for major building projects were still chosen by the monarch. Anecdotally, the architect who had been responsible for the maintenance of the Rue Le Peletier opera house after the death of François Debret in 1850, Charles Rohault de Fleury, was supposed to be in charge of the project. He had even studied it at Baron Haussmann's request. It seems that, in order to oust him, Eugène Viollet-le-Duc suggested the idea of a competition to Empress Eugénie. Against all expectations, the two rivals were eliminated in the first round, and Charles Garnier won the second round. He was thirty-five years old and had few built projects to his name.

Out of pique, Rohault de Fleury resigned as architect of the Salle Le Peletier and Garnier was appointed to the post. This was not incidental; the opera house was inspired by the general layout of the Théâtre Montansier, the work of the great neo-classical architect Victor Louis. Debret had notably reused the four pairs of columns supporting the auditorium and its dome. Garnier, who proclaimed a profound admiration for Louis, reused this layout in turn; he was also—more famously—inspired by the staircase of the Grand Théâtre de Bordeaux, another of Louis' masterpieces.

The foundation stone was laid on 21 July 1862 by Count Walewski, minister, son of Napoleon I and Countess Walewska. What better choice to preside over the ceremony than a man born of the greatest love story of the century? During the construction, as usual, there were many disputes between the architect and the ministers in charge and their departments: "It is by the thousands that one should count the reports we draft for civil servants who do not miss a chance to make

Count Alexandre Walewski in 1859, photograph by Eugène Disderi (private collection, Paris). Count Walewski (1810–1868), a state minister and responsible for the fine arts, presided over the jury that chose Charles Garnier in 1861; he laid the foundation stone the following year.

us write a volume to find out if a rat fell through the grating of a sewer," wrote Garnier (*Le Nouvel Opéra*, 171). Having betrayed the architect from the outset by cheating over the cost of the undertaking, "they" did not shy away from abandoning him in midstream in favour of other, more "political" projects, such as the Hôtel-Dieu. In a letter published in *Le Moniteur Officiel* on 2 August 1864, Napoleon III had warned his minister: "We should avoid being reproached for having spent millions on a theatre, when the foundation stone of the most popular hospital in Paris has not yet been laid." For which reason, from 1866, the Opéra budget was reduced drastically (cut in half in 1868). In 1903, in her *Notes pour la biographie de Charles Garnier*, Louise Garnier summed up ironically the imperial directives in the famous phrase: "The shelter for suffering will open before the temple of pleasure."

Nevertheless, the history of the construction enjoyed a few great moments.

Night of 26–27 August 1869

The Dance by Carpeaux, the controversial sculpture unveiled on the façade of the new Opéra a few weeks earlier, was damaged by the throwing of a bottle of ink.

"It seems that since the odes of Piron and the illustrations of Aretino, no human production has taken the pornographic idea so far! Lubricious old men stopped complacently in front of these figures of shameless women, young men smiled or made low jokes when they walked by the circle of frenzied dancers; mothers moved their sons away from the façade of the Opéra, and hypocrites obliquely lowered their eyes in the presence of this orgy of material forms. In fact, it was said that next to this vivid debauchery, the statues of all the Venuses and even that of the Hermaphrodite were objects of sanctity, and that their location in a church would seem more natural than the location of this accursed group on the façade of a theatre," wrote Garnier (*Le Nouvel Opéra*, 440) about the unveiling of Carpeaux's masterpiece on 25 July 1869.

The architect received a flurry of letters ("anonymous above all, it goes without saying"), as did the minister, the court, and the Senate. In one of them, the architect was asked the following question: "Is the Académie de Musique a brothel?" (Garnier, *Le Nouvel Opéra*, 440). It had not been the first time that *The Dance* had made trouble for him.

For Garnier, the principle that painters and sculptors had to respect above all else was harmony, the integration of their creations into the monument as a whole. One of the sculpted groups of the main façade that "the big boss", as his collaborators nicknamed him, cited was the well-named *Harmony* group by François Jouffroy. Of course, he acknowledged that its composition was somewhat banal and the execution lacking in character, "but in its type of artistic modesty this group is laid out in a way that fulfils all the desires of architects" (Garnier, *Le Nouvel Opéra*, 424). Jouffroy had agreed to be, Garnier acknowledges, the "collaborator in the great play that I was performing" (*Le Nouvel Opéra*, 424).

Garnier did not have the same satisfaction with the sculptors of the groups of the right avant-corps, especially with Jean-Baptiste Carpeaux, the childhood friend he affectionately called "the terror of architects". Garnier presented him with a small plaster model of the pedestal on which *The Dance* was going to be placed, a sketch of the silhouette, the required dimensions, etc. The first sketch by Carpeaux had nothing

Curious Onlookers in Front of The Dance *by Monsieur Carpeaux,* drawing by M. Miranda, 1869. This engraving, made for an unidentified newspaper, was reproduced in the special report on *The Dance* by Jean-Baptiste Carpeaux published by the Musée d'Orsay (Laure de Margerie, *La Danse de Carpeaux* [Paris: RMN, 1989], fig. 5, p. 13).

attacked: during the night of 26–27 August 1869, someone threw a bottle of ink at it. The damage was quickly repaired, but the emperor decided to remove the group and replace it with a chaster *Dance* commissioned from the sensible Charles Gumery—these decisions were confirmed by the Chamber after 1870. Only the death of Carpeaux, in October 1875, allowed his masterpiece to be saved.

More so than with Carpeaux (too independent), more so than with Gumery (too submissive), Garnier's collaboration with Jules Thomas demonstrated how, guided by the architect, the artists of the new Opéra produced decorations that were simultaneously new and rooted in tradition. To break out of the monochromy fashionable in France for over a century, Garnier wanted to revive the polychrome sculpture of the Romans that he had so admired in Italy. He asked Thomas to execute using this technique the two large caryatids supporting the door leading to the stalls, at the top of the grand staircase. First sketches: "They were two very charming figures, steady and well composed. Here was ancient Greece set on its prey" (Garnier, *Le Nouvel Opéra*, 156). And so, Garnier decided to pull out all the stops: "'My dear Thomas,' I said, 'do you remember Bernini's statues in Rome, the wild drapery, the outstretched arms, and the twisted legs? Well, I want you to do something even worse than that; I want you to do bad-taste Bernini! Is my cornice at the bottom in your way? Well, move your figures' hips; place the elbows on the bases of the columns; in short, make me some kind of moving marionette, and you will be on the right track.' I knew who I was talking to and you can be sure that I would never have said the same thing to Carpeaux, but I was certain that the faithful Thomas would try to do what I wanted and that at the same time his very refined talent would, in spite of himself, make him fight the exaggerations I had voiced" (Garnier, *Le Nouvel Opéra*, 157).

to do with either the programme or the subject; it was "Adam and Eve Given Ill Counsel by the Devil" according to Garnier and rejected. Garnier proposed new sketches and, this time, Carpeaux found his group. He could not refrain from adding a figure here and a figure there, "even adding, I think, one a day; so that at a certain point, there were seventeen of them" (Garnier, *Le Nouvel Opéra*, 432–35).

Some of them had to be removed, but the sculptor did not stop overdoing it. In the end, Garnier was resigned: "I decided, if Carpeaux did not want to listen to me, to let him do as he pleased. I found his model superb; I marvelled at his lively composition, at the thrilling modelling of his clay figures." Garnier appreciated talented mavericks. There was a compromise: *The Dance* has *only* nine figures, while its neighbour, *Lyric Drama* by Joseph Perraud, has four and Jouffroy's group three.

Far from ending with its unveiling to the public, on 25 July 1869, Garnier's troubles with this "very modern, lively, and distinctive work" (Garnier, *Le Nouvel Opéra*, 436) had only just begun, as it created an unforgettable scandal that resulted in it being

This example shows how these artists, guided by Garnier, gradually broke free of their models, but without losing the admirable technique they had acquired at the École des Beaux-Arts. From Greek harmony, Roman polychromy, and baroque movement the classical sculptor Thomas, spurred on by Garnier, invented something new. While Garnier did not singlehandedly reinvent polychrome statuary (Charles Cordier and Charles Simart had already made similar attempts), he had given it pride of place in a very prestigious undertaking. He thus helped create the fashion for colour from the Second Empire, with art nouveau and art deco.

The new Opéra should really be considered a "mutant". That is why it is unclassifiable and fascinating. Garnier mobilised the best of the art that had come before, drawing from it what he needed and rethinking it. He created a new synthesis, taking from classicism its grandeur and harmony, from the Italian Renaissance its humanism and colour, from the baroque its liveliness and movement, from Romanticism its dreamlike quality and freedom, from rationalism its sincerity and reason, making good use of everything that served his cause. The entire history of art was his palette, which he had in common with eclecticism. But he did not imitate it slavishly; he reworked everything and created his masterpiece, an opulent synthesis greater than the sum of its parts—and thus unclassifiable. In turn, this synthesis inspired and heralded the creative jubilation of art nouveau— its experimentation with materials, frenetic movement, and orgies of colour—and enthusiasm for the decorative arts. With its genuine volumes, which made clear the functions of the various parts of the monument, it also heralded functionalism and instigated the movement still in force today: an intellectual conception of art, reducing the artistic message to the essential.

The Second Empire had begun the new Opéra; the Republic finished it. Reluctantly.

29 October 1873

The fire that had ravaged the Opéra all night long had just been brought under control; all that remained were a few charred sections of wall. The heroism of the firefighters saved the neighbourhood, but sadly one of them died.

Work on the future Palais Garnier limped along, completely unnoticed and interrupted once a year by the budgetary dispute, then the "temporary" opera house in the Rue Le Peletier burnt down. After fifty-three years of existence, it was bound to happen: at the time, in Europe, the average lifespan of theatres was thirteen years, mainly because of fires. At dawn, nothing remained of this cultural centre, which had played such an important role in French artistic life. It was there that Romantic ballet and French "grand opera" had bloomed.

After this disaster, Garnier was ordered to finish the new Opéra urgently; he was given eighteen months and 6.9 million francs. On 30 December 1874, after frenzied work, Garnier delivered a building, parts of which were barely dry and others unfinished. At the time of the inauguration on 5 January 1875, neither the smoking room nor the Glacier (refreshment room) was installed. The smoking room, assigned to the museum at the same time as the west pavilion, was never put in; the Glacier was, but in less ambitious form. However, the elements that were not finished before the inauguration for want of time or means and those added later (the ceiling by Marc Chagall, essentially) were peripheral. The foremost merit of this extraordinary building is its unity. The Palais Garnier is a rather exceptional case in the history of architecture:

The caryatids by Jules Thomas in the grand staircase. They are not really "marionettes", but admirable works in marble and bronze.

it is the work of a single man who, from start to finish, designed everything, chose everything, and executed everything, or almost everything. Garnier was proud of this all-encompassing paternity: "There will not be the tiniest space in the building that I cannot patent," he wrote (*Le Nouvel Opéra*, 164). Not that he had worked alone; but nearly all the artists who had collaborated on the new Opéra were chosen by Garnier amongst his former fellow students at the Villa Medici, who were educated at the École des Beaux-Arts before winning the famous Prix de Rome, beginning with his assistant, Victor Louvet (grand prize for architecture, 1850). The principal painters of the monument had studied there: the painters of the grand foyer, Paul Baudry (grand prize, 1850), Félix Barrias (grand prize, 1844), and Élie Delaunay (grand prize, 1856); the painter of the auditorium ceiling, Eugène Lenepveu (grand prize, 1847, he headed the French Academy in Rome from 1872 to 1878); the painter of the ceiling panels of the grand staircase, Isidore Pils, had been awarded the grand prize in 1838, while Gustave Boulanger, the painter of the Foyer de la Danse, won in 1849.

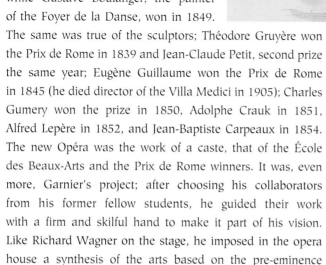

The same was true of the sculptors; Théodore Gruyère won the Prix de Rome in 1839 and Jean-Claude Petit, second prize the same year; Eugène Guillaume won the Prix de Rome in 1845 (he died director of the Villa Medici in 1905); Charles Gumery won the prize in 1850, Adolphe Crauk in 1851, Alfred Lepère in 1852, and Jean-Baptiste Carpeaux in 1854. The new Opéra was the work of a caste, that of the École des Beaux-Arts and the Prix de Rome winners. It was, even more, Garnier's project; after choosing his collaborators from his former fellow students, he guided their work with a firm and skilful hand to make it part of his vision. Like Richard Wagner on the stage, he imposed in the opera house a synthesis of the arts based on the pre-eminence of architecture. Like poetry or dance combined with music

in Wagner's *Gesamtkunstwerk*, painting and sculpture were supposed to blend into the architecture of this monument.

Garnier commandeered not only painters and sculptors, but also stonecutters, casters, and tapestry-makers, bringing together various trades to serve a single objective: opera, the lyric art. Or, better, to serve the pleasure of the audience. At the Opéra, the audience came to enjoy the spectacle of a world created by man for the pleasure of man. Garnier understood that the monument housing the spectacle was part of the response to the quest for the Holy Grail of dreams. Opera is a "fairy kingdom", in the fine words of Voltaire. The opera house itself, the stone alter ego of the lyric art, should also be a fairy kingdom or, at least, a setting worthy of one.

Charles Garnier's opera house is a good response to a real question—perpetually asked: how does one, now and then, give man the illusion that his dreams are being realised, so that he will be able to bear the rest of the time, when they are not? That is when the architect is crucial. Leading all his people, Garnier composed an opera of forms and matter for the pleasure of the audience. He was the composer of an opera that was one of a kind: an opera in stone. His palace took on the characteristics of a poetic universe; all the complementary spaces of the theatre were developed in a way hitherto unknown, and are larger and more splendid than the auditorium, which is no more than the heart of the sanctuary. The entire building is theatre. The spectators themselves become actors and perform, directed by the demiurge Garnier as soon as they walk on to the disguised stage that is the grand staircase.

The pre-eminence of the space reserved for spectators, which struck commentators, is clearly not gratuitous. So far,

Monsieur Garnier, Architect of the Opéra, drawing by Charles Giraud from a series of 51 lithographs, *Théâtre national de l'Opéra*, 1899 (private collection, Paris). Charles Garnier had died the previous year, on 3 August 1898. But for Charles Giraud, he still made his stone instrument sing. Finely observed.

it has above all been "explained" in terms of social considerations: the Palais Garnier was thought to be the "worldly cathedral" of which Théophile Gautier spoke (about the Salle Le Peletier, in reality), the mirror of Second Empire society (of the Third Republic, in fact), a society so superficial and so bourgeois that the staircase and the foyers are its theatre, etc. None of this is untrue, but it amounts to mistaking the effect for the causes in a recent "culturally correct" interpretation. It is because Garnier wanted to *enlist* the spectators that they got involved, as human vanity always does whenever the opportunity arises.

In this cocoon outside of ordinary space and time reigns the world of legend, the indolent nymph and the lascivious faun; allusions to the outside world were only allowed in the allegorical mode. The stage and the theatre thus together met—and still meet today—one of man's eternal needs. The dream world that the spectator comes to seek is found as much in the monument as in the spectacle that it contains. The Palais Garnier is a waking dream in architecture, like opera (the lyric art) is a waking dream in music. The public success, which has never waned, is not surprising; this success means that, Bastille or not, a night at the opera remains for many, including the young, a night at the Palais Garnier.

15 October 1881

Monsieur Cochery, minister of Post and Telegraphs, invited officials and scholars to a gala evening at the Opéra to see Aida *by Giuseppe Verdi, marking the closing of the electricity exhibition at the Palais de l'Industrie.*

The highlight of the evening was not Verdi's opera; once again, it was the theatre, which became a showcase for all the recent advances in electric lighting—those made in the two previous years were dazzling: at the exhibition itself, forty or so systems were presented. There were not that many at the Palais Garnier, but the three main technological families were present. The arc lamps highlighted

the architecture of the grand staircase; in the auditorium, the Yablochkov candles (named after the Russian physicist who had invented them a few years earlier) made all the facets of the theatre gleam and glitter; incandescent lamps (the ancestors of today's lamps, since this system prevailed) illuminated the grand foyer, the auditorium chandelier, and the small side salons of the foyer. The experiment was fascinating, even though the white light was not very popular as it was considered too harsh and blinding. While the stage was not dealt with as a priority—and yet,

The Opéra Lighting Board, anonymous engraving published in *Trucs et Décors* by Georges Moynet (Paris: Librairie illustrée, 1893). Garnier placed the lighting board for the theatre, stage, and auditorium under the proscenium, in the centre. Thus, in Gaston Leroux's novel, the Phantom of the Opera is able to put out all the lights in the theatre by drugging the electricians and abduct the beautiful singer Christine Daaé in the middle of a performance.

The iron structure of the theatre being assembled, photograph by Delmaet and Durandelle taken on 10 May 1865 (BMO, Paris). The trusses of the auditorium floor follow the form of the future vault of the season-ticket holders' entrance hall. The metal frame of the walls is under construction, and the first two levels of the trusses of the floors of the boxes are already in place.

The twelve piers supporting the auditorium of the Palais Garnier. Charles Garnier, *Le Nouvel Opéra de Paris*, volume 1, plate 15: "Detail of the auditorium ceiling." In this engraving, the twelve piers that surround and support the auditorium and everything above it are depicted in plan. It can clearly be seen how each pier is made up of four cast-iron columns, two large ones, which bear the weight of the superstructures, and two smaller ones, which support all the floors and galleries, embedded in masonry bases. Each column, an assembly of six elements, is 20 metres high.

it was a matter of urgency there, because of the risk of fire—the electrical fittings of the Palais Garnier were installed in 1887, when a complete network, supplied by a "plant" in the basement, was finished. Paris was on schedule; La Scala was completely fitted out in 1891, as was Bayreuth for the *Ring* of 1896.

But why the blazes did Garnier wait so long and why did he not fit out the building from its inauguration? He answered this question, noting that in 1875 the lighting technique had not yet been perfected, even though all signs were that it would be a success; the use of electricity was thus restricted to bells and certain theatrical effects, after a long period of testing. Electricity had already made an appearance at the Salle Le Peletier on 16 April 1849, during a dance by Dutch skaters in Giacomo Meyerbeer's *Le Prophète* where, according to one poetical reviewer, it "projected into the dull sky of a winter morning the pale radiance of a phantom star" (*Exposition universelle de 1900*, report by C. Raynaud, 159). Despite its limited scope, this technological first was hailed by Frédéric Chopin, who had extolled in a letter the appearance of "a sun at the Opéra".

Otherwise, gas still reigned supreme at the new Opéra with the help of—Garnier being Garnier—the latest technological developments. The lighting board was the centrepiece of the installation, stage and auditorium. The lighting board, the console that controls the lights in a theatre, originated in the use of gas lighting: in grouping at a single point the valves controlling the gas lamps of the theatre, a single man could instantaneously produce all the required lighting effects. The lighting board, as such, was developed in the 1860s by Lecoq, a firm whose services Garnier used for the new Opéra; he improved the system by placing the lighting board at the centre of the proscenium, enabling the chief electrician to keep an eye on everything from a "box" near that of the prompter. The electrical fittings of the theatre were refurbished several times, notably in 1936 and 1971; the lighting board was then installed in its current location, at the centre of the third-balcony boxes.

As shown by this example, Garnier kept tabs on all technological advances but did not take risks—dangerous in a building of this importance. He followed the "gentle slope" of progress. On the whole, the new Opéra was an extremely innovative project. For example, the auditorium is, at first sight, a construction of marble, stone, and stucco swathed in gold and velvet—a classic construction. Not really; it is above all an iron construction. Even though barely any metal can be seen—the armature of the chandelier, a few door handles perhaps—the opera house is entirely built using this advanced technology, which then spread over in Paris, from the Eiffel Tower to the Grand Palais, and around the world.

The technical problems were immense: the wall of a proscenium theatre had to have several openings providing access to the boxes and allowing for the installation of heating and ventilation shafts, etc. The bearing surface was thus limited. The location of the season-ticket holders' entrance hall directly below further complicated things. The number of piers supporting the whole had to be small (twelve only), and they had to be reduced in surface area (1 square metre each), rise over 25 metres high, and bear a considerable

Inauguration of the new auditorium ceiling by Marc Chagall.
The artist notably stated: "I wanted to reflect, up high, as in a mirror,
in a bouquet the dreams, the creations of the actors and musicians;
bear in mind that below, the colours of the clothing of the spectators
were moving. To sing like a bird, without theory or method"
(Les Peintures de l'Opéra de Paris [Paris: Arthena, 1980], 187).

total load. Twelve piers of one square metre each to support the entire auditorium and everything above it—that was the challenge Garnier faced.

The architect found the solution to this challenge in a technique from the flourishing industrial construction sector: the combination of hollow cast-iron columns with metal lintels. The twelve piers each comprise four cast-iron columns, two bearing the floors of the boxes, amphitheatre, and corridors serving them, the two others bearing the rest—that is, everything above the auditorium (the ceiling, the chandelier and its counterweights, the dome—particularly its stone wall, 10 metres high—etc.). Garnier chose to separate them in order to limit the vibrations transmitted by the floors, especially on evening when balls were held. The four columns were reinforced with wrought-iron struts, all embedded in Burgundian brick and cement.

Even the floor of the auditorium is held up by iron. There is metal everywhere; iron architecture disguised with a bit of masonry and a lot of decoration, such is the heart of the Opéra. A world première. Garnier later teamed up with Gustave Eiffel, a few years his junior; together they built the Observatoire de Nice (1880–92); in 1894, when the Opéra ateliers burnt down, they joined forces once more to rebuild them in Boulevard Berthier.

The Palais Garnier is indisputably a modern building.

In 1960 Minister of Culture André Malraux made a spectacular gesture, which was considered daring at the time. A media coup at the moment when the media were taking over the world. A sacrilege, too, as Chagall's ceiling covered the work of Eugène Lenepveu (an artist who was out of favour at the time, like all the 19th-century academic painters, but not for long); a sacrilege, too, with regard to Garnier's principle of harmony, a principle that all the artists had respected, even, to a certain extent, Carpeaux. But Garnier was no longer there to watch over the unity of his palace of dreams. Undeniably, Chagall's ceiling made the Palais Garnier fashionable again. Just as, twenty-two years later, Daniel Buren's columns would let Parisians rediscover a forgotten Palais-Royal when they replaced the car park that dishonoured its courtyard. And just as Ieoh Ming Pei's pyramid ensured the Louvre of global media coverage in 1989. Whatever one may think of their artistic merits, these three gestures were undeniably successful communications operations.

The three interventions represented both a break with the past and continuation of tradition. As for Chagall's ceiling, it is an undeniable break in the unity of the auditorium. However, in many respects, it is the continuation of the work of Garnier, whose *Le Nouvel Opéra* Chagall had read attentively. First of all, he carried on, with his "admirable prismatic colours"— in the words of André Breton—the reintroduction of colour, which was so important to Garnier. Chagall himself had discovered his gift for colour in Paris: "In Russia, everything was dark, brown, grey. When I came to France, I was struck by the shimmering colours and the play of light. And I found what I had been blindly seeking, this refinement of matter

Pelléas et Mélisande
by Claude Debussy,
detail of the ceiling
by Marc Chagall.
Predominant colour: blue.
Lying alongside the head
of the nymph Clytia
sculpted by Joseph-Adolphe-
Alexandre Walter and
Maximilien Bourgeois,
Mélisande is observed
by Pelléas from a window
in a playful reversal of roles.
According to Jacques
Lasseigne, Chagall gave
Pelléas the features of
André Malraux. Above them,
a crowned head watches—
probably Prince Golaud.

Roméo et Juliette
by Hector Berlioz, detail of
the ceiling by Marc Chagall.
Predominant colour: green.
The embracing couple
is surrounded by a horse's
head and a "figure sign",
reminiscent of Chagall's 1911
painting *The Holy Coachman*,
that ends in an "aureole"
framing their faces.

and uninhibited colour" (*Marc Chagall*, exh. cat. [Paris: Musée des Arts Décoratifs, 1959]; Marc Chagall's comments on his painting *The Musician*, no. 4, p. 88).

Moreover, Chagall's ceiling completes the Palais Garnier "pantheon" of famous composers, by adding the architect's "forgotten" contemporaries (in 1875, Verdi was the only living composer represented by a statue), such as Berlioz (there has been, however, a bust of the composer in the corridors since 1885) and Wagner (a bust was commissioned in 1903), and a few major composers of the late 19th century and 20th century. What's more, Chagall evokes these composers in an "Olympus" of characters from their operas; "Olympus" was the generic term Garnier used for theatre ceilings.

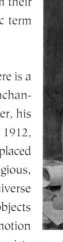

Chagall was a lyrical painter and there is a profound sympathy for Garnier's enchanted palace in his ceiling; like Garnier, his painting was, as Apollinaire put it in 1912, "super-natural" (this term was later replaced by "surrealist"). For Chagall's religious, even mystical spirit, the entire universe was moved by love; creatures and objects were carried along in an absolute motion without top or bottom, gravity or resistance—the ideal thing for an opera house ceiling. Like the architect, the painter dreamed of total theatre, which did not distinguish between setting and plot. He demonstrated this as a young man in Vitebsk, during his spell as director of the academy of fine arts of his hometown and when he helped renovate the Moscow State Jewish Theatre between 1919 and 1921.

The work was painted between January and August 1964 on a dozen canvas panels and a central panel, mounted on a plastic armature—240 square metres in total. As for the original ceiling by Eugène Lenepveu, it is still in place, underneath Chagall's ceiling; the model may be viewed at the Musée d'Orsay.

Portrait of Charles Garnier by Paul Baudry, oil on canvas (Musée d'Orsay, Paris). This portrait is thought to have been painted by Baudry in 1864 while Carpeaux was sculpting his famous bust. "His playfulness and fondness for practical jokes would categorise him as one of the Romantic daubers, and his eternal pea jacket, turned-down collar, string tie, and shaggy hat showed no pretension to worldly elegance. He loved life and laughter, punned with the naivety of a child, often used Rabelaisian language, was unaware of the existence of Schopenhauer, and was upset when life required him to take precautions" (Frantz Jourdain, *Au pays du souvenir* [Paris: Gres et Cie, 1922], 42).

"The style I use is my own"

The work of a man's life, the work of a single man who conceived and designed it down to the last detail, including the works of his many collaborators, the Palais Garnier is difficult to place in a classical category of art history. In her *Notes pour la biographie de Charles Garnier*, written in 1903 and kept in the Opéra library-museum, Garnier's widow credited the architect with a retort—probably apocryphal—supposedly addressed to Empress Eugénie. The scene was said to have taken place in the Tuileries, when Garnier was presenting his project to Napoleon III. The empress, whose protégé Viollet-le-Duc had lost the competition, entered the room, looked at the plans, and said disdainfully: "What is this style? It's not a style! It's not Greek, not Louis XVI, not even Louis XV!" Garnier was said to have rather curtly replied: "No, those styles are outmoded. It's Napoleon III style! And you're complaining!"

Louise Garnier's account dates from forty years after the fact. In his writings, Charles Garnier had never mentioned "Napoleon III style", neither in relation to the work of his colleagues nor to describe his own. On the other hand, whenever he was asked about style, he proudly gave the best answer: "The style I use is my own" (Charles Garnier, *À travers les arts, causeries et mélanges* [Paris: Hachette, 1869], 68–69).

It was the only response worthy of a masterpiece.

A closer look

**The ideal view
of the south façade.**
A façade that is both classical
and baroque. Classical
because it was inspired
by Claude Perrault's Louvre
colonnade (1667) and
Ange-Jacques Gabriel's
Garde-Meuble (1768);
baroque in the exuberance
of its decoration and
in its polychromy. It was
slightly thrown off balance
by the addition of an attic
that was too high; during
construction, it replaced
the balustrade of the original
project to counterbalance
the rapid growth of the
building's surroundings.
Garnier provides the solution:
"I can see the attic get
smaller and revert to better
proportions. To do so,
I only need to stand more or
less at the foot of the grand
perron, and preferably
at one of the sides.
Moreover, in my opinion,
this standpoint is among
those where one should
stand to study the building
from one of its best angles.
It all holds together, and the
projections, very pronounced
in this three-quarter view,
give the façade great
power and movement"
(*Le Nouvel Opéra*, 29).

ACADEMIE · NATIONALE · DE · MUSIQUE

BEETHOVEN · 1827   1756 · MOZART · 1791   1774 · SPONTINI

Central bay of the façade. In Garnier's day, distinguished architecture was neo-classical and monochrome. Garnier had discovered the baroque and colour in Italy; he injected movement, variety, and even whimsy into a noble classical plan. This was surprising, even shocking, and the architect had to justify his decisions. To a journalist who remarked: "It's the outfit of a fishwife who would like to make her entrance in society", he replied: "I imagined that a theatre should look cheerier than a prison, as a woman at a ball should look smarter than a slattern doing the washing-up" (Garnier, *Le Nouvel Opéra*, 22).

West pediment.
The south façade is
an iconostasis; eighteen
sculptors worked on it.
Two magnificent pediments
frame it. The left pediment is
topped by Charles Gumery's
Harmony—7.5 metres high.
Garnier kept wondering:
"Are they too big?
Are they too small?"
Harmony holding her
lyre up is flanked by two
seated Fames. The upper
frieze is punctuated by
fifty-three theatrical masks
by Jean-Baptiste Klagmann—
it was his final work.
The pediment features,
linked by Garnier
in a prophetic vision,
Architecture and Industry
by Jean-Claude Petit.
Very refined, the symbolic
objects are gilt. In the screen
wall oculus is Gustave-Grégoire
Evrard's bust of Rossini.
On the right, on the attic,
one of the seven bas-reliefs
adorned with children
by Louis Villeminot.

Preceding pages

Paris at night: the Pantheon, the Eiffel Tower, and the Grand Palais.
In the foreground, an allegory of Fame from Charles Gumery's *Harmony* group. From the roof of the Opéra, one of the most beautiful views of the city.
An opera house is the kingdom of the imagination; it communicates with hell via its subterranean spaces peopled with phantoms, and with heaven via its gilt domes and solar divinities. Up there, even Fame, which the ancients, more sensibly perhaps, depicted as a monster with a hundred mouths, a hundred ears, and a hundred eyes, becomes an amiable winged young woman holding a simple trumpet. It is understandable that, in *The Phantom of the Opera*, the singer Christine Daaé and her beloved take refuge there to exchange confidences and vows of love.

The Dance
by Jean-Baptiste Carpeaux, Euville limestone replica produced by Paul Belmondo in 1964. The star group, not only of the principal façade, but also of the entire monument. And yet the competition was strong: over a hundred sculptors worked on this veritable museum of the sculpture of the period. The original is now in the Musée d'Orsay, sheltered from pollution.

1756 · MOZART + 1791

Bas-relief with children by Louis Villeminot, detail. Méry-sur-Oise limestone. On a gold mosaic ground, two children hold a heavy garland of flowers and fruits topped by a green Swedish marble medallion. Five of these bas-reliefs adorn the central section of the attic, alternating with four high reliefs by Jacques Maillet bearing red porphyry medallions. These medallions feature the gold letters "N" and "E"; they stand for "Napoleon" and "Emperor"— not, as legend has it, for "Eugénie".

Mozart by Félix Chabaud. Leaf gilt electroplated bronze. Garnier loved music— this is one of the keys to his opera house's success. On three of the façades, he arranged a "pantheon" of thirty-one composers and two librettists; for lack of a consensus of experts, he ended up picking them himself, an eclectic and personal selection. They are arranged in chronological order of birth, starting with Wolfgang Amadeus Mozart in the centre. Garner commissioned this bust from his former fellow student at the Villa Medici, the sculptor Chabaud, who produced a multitude of decorative figures for the interior and exterior of the new Opéra. Exceptionally, the two masks inspired by classical theatre flanking the oculus are by Ernest Barrias.

The ceiling of the loggia.
A masterpiece and technical tour de force that was half a century ahead of its time. To prevent the succession of flat arches from exerting dangerous thrust on the façade, Garnier enclosed them in stone frames hung from girders with iron rods, like an everyday plaster double ceiling. Like the red sandstone lintels, instead of supporting they are supported. This technical inventiveness and the combination of a wide variety of materials resulted in Garnier's work being described as ikebana: a bit of stone, a lot of marble, metal everywhere—exposed, concealed—and mosaics. Mosaic—borrowed from Italian art, and an ancient idea with a bright future—was reintroduced into France by Garnier. It flourished with art nouveau.

The loggia at night.
Another idea of Italian origin,
the loggia is protected from
bad weather by screen walls,
a sort of marble and gold
drapery of times of legend—
a worthy shelter for an
assembly of the gods.
Running along the entire
length of the grand foyer, it is
the balcony of gala evenings.

Following pages :

**From the lyre
of Millet's Apollo**
at the top of the building
(69 metres high), Garnier
wanted gold to glitter all over
the domes and rooftops,
extending to the façade.
Too much gold? As can
be seen in this photograph,
the architect had to abandon
most of his planned exterior
gilding after the defeat of 1870.

Eagles by Auguste Cain adorning the top of the Head of State Pavilion. Electroplated bronze. After the defeat of 1870 and the fall of the empire, Garnier had to defend all the emblems connected to the fallen regime, considering that they were part of the history of the building— and of history per se.

These are not the only animals living on the rooftops of the Opéra. There are other, live animals: a colony of kestrels has taken up residence in the dome; the famous bees, whose seven hives were placed on the roof by the management, produce honey that is very much in demand amongst music lovers and tourists.

Pegasus by Eugène Lequesne. Electroplated bronze by Léopold Oudry. The mythical winged horse of Parnassus rears up atop the gable wall, whose air of grandeur it affirms. Garnier: "Horses' heads are enormous in relation to their bodies (that is how Phidias did things), and the hind legs are short

and squat. The arbitrary construction of the horse gives the group a distinct and architectural character. The legs, reduced in this way, solidly support the trunk of the horse—without leaving gaps that, seen from a distance, would inevitably produce gauntness, and the large head, vigorous and confidently

modelled, complete the contours of the horse with decisive lines. The wings are also vigorous and understated, and the whole, treated in an ornamental rather than natural style, harmonises perfectly with the real ornaments and the rigid lines of the architecture" (*Le Nouvel Opéra*, 112).

Season-ticket holders' rotunda. Originally, the façade was neither the only entrance nor the most important. The fashionable entrances were the side pavilions, reserved for season-ticket holders to the east and the head of state to the west. The Season-Ticket Holders' Pavilion was used until the Second World War. Its ground floor creates the illusion of a succession of caves.

Located directly underneath the auditorium, this famous rotunda has a relatively low ceiling; but Garnier balanced its volume with a masterly portico of sixteen fluted columns in Sampans marble from the Jura with bases and capitals in Carrara marble. Like all the mosaics of the public areas of the Palais Garnier, the superb marble floral motifs on the floors were executed by two Italian mosaic setters living in Paris, Cristofoli and Mazzioli. Most of the original furniture is gone, but the Sèvres vases designed by Garnier are still in the four side niches. The mirrors of the vault were added later.

Vault of the season-ticket holders' rotunda: Garnier's signature.
In this rotunda, Garnier's decorative magic begins to take hold of the spectators. They have been discreetly warned; in the centre of the vault is an extraordinary zodiac sculpted by Félix Chabaud, a zodiac that is also a compass, both slightly unconventional. From this point, the Opéra imposes its time and space, becoming, for the space of an evening, the world—that of the wizard Garnier. This is where, logically enough, he appended his signature in Arabic characters, which were cryptic and therefore magical: Jean-Louis-Charles Garnier, architect, 1861–75. This impertinent act was significant at a time when architects did not sign their works. Garnier helped introduce the custom.

Marble paving, ticket check.
Through this entrance, one enters a world whose laws are different from those of everyday life, a world in which all is peace (order), luxury (marble), and pleasure (shimmering colours). This is expressed by the superb paving. Here the devotee proves that he is ready to abandon—for a short while—ordinary life to enter the extraordinary. Garnier thought that the paving was "cut and laid with a rare perfection" and paid a glowing tribute to Verne, a marble setter from the firm of Drouet and Langlois, who oversaw the work. By its very architectural structure, the ticket check also performs the mission of preparing the spectator for the dazzling discovery to come, the grand staircase and the ascension to pleasure. It was in order to set off the staircase that Garnier designed the ticket check so low.

The Pythia
by Marcello. Bronze.
The fact that season-ticket holders were welcomed by the Pythia seems natural: the priestess of Apollo delivered the oracles of the god at Delphi. Of course, one could have one's doubts about the suitability of such a figure. Sitting above a chasm from which prophetic vapours rose, she would enter into trances and wail. Even worse, Marcello's Pythia is from India, a kind of gypsy. This highly exotic Pythia is worlds away from the classical canons of beauty. But this masterpiece quivering with life, strength, and frenzy embodies the forbidden passions of the knowing women who came from elsewhere: Medea, Kundry, Azucena, Preziosilla, Ulrica, Carmen— an allegory of the hidden side of opera. Garnier designed the two bronze candelabra flanking the statue.

The grand staircase from the season-ticket holders' entrance.
Garnier was a forerunner in the field of the psychology of the environment; his architecture was to a great extent conceived with its effect on the spectator in mind. He thought that the higher a space was, the greater its symbolism; it is thus not fortuitous that the staircase is the highest space (30 metres) in the entire monument. Here according to Garnier, is the best vantage point: from the vestibule containing *The Pythia*, the staircase to its fullest extent, a sort of immense marble and gold Ali Baba's cave crowned by Isidore Pils's paintings, with *The Triumph of Apollo* in pride of place. This is where the grand spectacle of a world that is not quite our own really begins.

"Grand staircase this, grand staircase that— to think there is not one good journalist kind enough to take it down a peg or two! To think I have nothing to defend, that they have left me here, stewing in my bliss" (Garnier, *Le Nouvel Opéra*, 152). Garnier's mock lament notwithstanding, the truth is that the staircase was unanimously admired. A majestic setting, grand perspectives, beautiful materials, perfect shapes: everything heralds the bliss that the imagination has the right to expect when entering a royal palace—or when going up this staircase. Garnier dreamed of being, for one evening only, the director of the Opéra. And of giving a performance in its grand staircase.

Base of the grand staircase torchères.
One of Garnier's principal ideas was to reintroduce colour into architecture. Here, colour reigns supreme through marble. The grand staircase is a dazzling study in fine marble work that earned its composer the nickname "the Veronese of architecture". Reds, yellows, greens, whites, greys, violets, pinks, opalescent marble, mottled marble, and a variety of others. A celebration of marble.

The columns of the grand staircase.
At that time, few quarries could supply blocks of this size at a reasonable price in the range of colours Garnier wanted. The architect chose this attractive blood-red marble flecked with ochre. The Sarrancolin quarry in the Hautes-Pyrénées from where these thirty monolithic columns come is still active, and has been since the Middle Ages; in Garnier's days, it was worked by the Dervillé company, which took a great risk when it accepted the order. Five metres high, these columns cost 4,933 gold francs each (45,000 euros). The bases and capitals are in white marble from Saint-Béat, Haute-Garonne.

**Garnier designed
the grand staircase
like a theatre.**
This is evident when it is
compared to the architect's
model in the Grand Théâtre
de Bordeaux by Victor Louis.
Each floor is endowed
with balconies that allow
the audience to admire
the spectacle of high society
and take part in it.
On the four sides of the
reception floor are veritable
prosceniums in precious
marbles. On the second and
third floors, the balconies
are adorned with attractive
bronze railings designed by
Garnier. The main staircase
of the Opéra thus becomes
a stage surrounded by
a genuine theatre, whose
every "box" is a secondary
stage. While the overall
structure is classical, Garnier
reworked Louis' staircase
to create a baroque
theatre-staircase.

**Reception floor,
jasper columns of the
secondary staircases.**
Garnier was always
on the lookout for ways
to enrich his artistic palette.
In the early 1860s, a deposit
of admirable jasper was
discovered in Saint-Gervais,
on the Fayet road.
This Mont-Blanc jasper is a
very hard stone of the agate
family and is red, yellow,
or green, uniform or flecked;
this was the first time
it was used in Paris. Note
the elegance of the bronze
lamp lighting the staircase.
Garnier designed dozens
of variations of them.

Box between the columns and its salon.
In the past, the relationship to the performance was very different to that of today; rented by the year, a box was like a corner of the family sitting room, from one side of which a performance could be watched if it was deemed worthy of interest; otherwise, one came and went, visited, chatted, ate, and drank. The Palais Garnier retains a reflection of these practices, which began to change while it was being built; the boxes and *baignoires* (boxes at stalls level) of the four floors each have their own "salon", constituting terraces of these salons open to the auditorium. On the other side of the auditorium, the proscenium box that must have been that of the emperor, and Auguste Rubé and Philippe Chaperon's *trompe-l'œil* stage curtain, one of the most beautiful ever painted.

Exterior of the upper circle between the columns: *Feline Head* by Jules Corboz. In the Duchesse de Guermantes' *baignoire* at the Opéra, Marcel Proust saw "the Assembly of the Gods in the act of contemplating the spectacle of mankind, beneath a crimson canopy, in a clear lighted space, between two pillars of Heaven" (*Remembrance of Things Past*, trans. C. K. Scott Moncrieff). The auditorium was designed to stage the spectators, especially the women spectators. Garnier designed it as a showcase and chose red because "the rosy reflections on women's faces and shoulders make them look younger and more radiant" (Charles Garnier, *Le Théâtre* [Arles: Actes Sud, 1990], 166). The colour has since become that of opera houses. As for the gilding, it was executed using a very economical old technique that Garnier discovered in Italy: *à effet* gilding. Instead of using full gilding—covering the entire surface with gold leaf—gold paint is applied to the shadows, and the lit sections are heightened with gold.

**The auditorium
from grand circle box 39.**
"Too much gold!
Too much gold! That's what
they are saying about the
Opéra auditorium and foyer,
and the sums swallowed up
and the abundance
of the streams of gold
I poured into my bottomless
pit were calculated
with dread" (Garnier,
Le Nouvel Opéra, 79–83).
Garnier promptly refuted this.
The "full" gilding at the Salle
Le Peletier had cost
53,000 francs (500,000 euros)
for a surface area
of 1,700 square metres;
the *à effet* gilding of the new
theatre cost 47,520 francs
for a surface area
of 4,400 square metres.
"That is how things are
judged and people accused,"
Garnier scornfully concluded.

The auditorium ceiling.
Twelve canvas panels
and a circular central
panel mounted on a plastic
armature (approximately
240 square metres in total).
Signed on the central
and main panels:
Chagall Marc 1964.
Half a century later,
the emotion aroused by
this "birdsong" still inspires
impassioned comments.

**The auditorium
from the stage.**

**The stage from the
auditorium;** in the background,
the Foyer de la Danse.
The Foyer de la Danse is
separated from the stage by
two curtains, a velvet one and
an iron one, both of which may
be opened; some 15 metres
of depth can thus be added,
making for an impressive

50-metre perspective.
In the foreground, the
lambrequin framing the upper
section of the stage; like the
stage curtain, it is the work of
Rubé and Chaperon. Garnier
played a large role in its
design and chose to inscribe
in the central cartouche
the arms of the Sun King
and the year of the foundation
of the Académie Royale
de Musique: *Anno 1669.*

The stage.
"We are both
in a jacquard loom
and on the deck
of a large ship" (Garnier,
Le Nouvel Opéra, 215)—
a ship from the age
of sails. The stage
equipment was
designed for the lavish
operas of the time
of the theatre's
construction.

Mlle Guimard
by Jules Cambos.
Marble, signed, dated 1881.
Kept in a princely fashion
by powerful protectors,
the dancer Marie-Madeleine
Guimard lived almost exactly
on the site of the future
stage of the Palais Garnier,
in a splendid mansion
decorated by Jean-Honoré
Fragonard where she
received high society.
She reigned over the Opéra
for years. On a day she refused
to dance, she was told that
the minister would be angry:
"The minister wants me
to dance? He had better
watch out; I could
have him sacked!"
Ruined by her extravagance,
she put her lovely mansion
up to be raffled. Sophie
Arnould claimed that
she died "on an honourable
deathbed"; but she settled
down, marrying a dancer
fifteen years her junior.

The Foyer de la Danse,
a strategic place.
From 1770, a special foyer
allowed privileged spectators
to meet the performers.
Then the Foyer de la Danse
allowed dancers to take
over. Over the years,

it became an institution
for Parisian *haute galanterie*,
whose habitués also
talked about politics or
business with those from
the same social circles.
Garnier thus gave it a prime
location: at the back of

the stage, in direct line with
the auditorium. He endowed
it with majestic volumes and
sumptuous decoration that
he later judged harshly: "The
legs of a giraffe supporting
the body of an elephant"
(*Le Nouvel Opéra*, 88).

It was considered
scandalous for other
reasons: an immense mirror,
banquettes upholstered with
lilac velvet, and, above all,
Gustave Boulanger's
paintings depicting dance
in all its facets.

The foyers.
The curtains of the grand foyer, recently refurbished, open on to the avant-foyer; in the background, the grand staircase. The size and luxuriousness of the public areas of the Palais Garnier struck all commentators. Up to the early 19th century, set changes took place in full view of the audience and the performance ran without interruption; as the auditorium was not heated, the audience could go warm up in the "foyer", a fairly small space serving as a café or even a gambling joint. Beginning in the 1820s, the set designs became more elaborate, and intervals appeared; longer and longer, they became as important a moment to get right as the acts. Garnier designed his public areas like another performance— a world of poetry.

Right-hand page

The grand foyer.
Between December 1875 and July 1876, the American novelist Henry James wrote for the *New York Tribune*. This is what he had to say about the grand foyer: "If the world were ever reduced to the dominion of a single gorgeous potentate, the foyer would do very well for his throne room."

Following pages

Ceilings and ceiling panels of the grand foyer decorated by Paul Baudry, 1865–74. Three ceilings, twelve ceiling panels, eight Muses, and ten medallions; thirty-three canvases, 371 square metres. According to Henry James, Baudry's frescoes "are very noble and beautiful, and the most interesting things in the building. You manage to perceive that much of this is exquisite, and you cannot help feeling a certain admiration for a building which can afford to consign such costly work to the reign of cobwebs."
To this criticism, which James was not the only one to voice, Garnier replied that a high room naturally leads one to raise one's eyes and that he had made the foyer as high as he could to lead the gaze towards the vault: "If Baudry's paintings had been executed on ceiling panels that were much lower than the actual ones, people might well have had a better view of them, but there can be no doubt that they would have looked at them less well" (*Le Nouvel Opéra*, 119).

The avant-foyer, the triumph of mosaic.
From the beginning of construction, Garnier wanted to make mosaic, which he had discovered in Italy, part of his artistic palette. He first had a few Italian craftsmen— attracted to Paris— make the large lyres with laurel leaves of the stage walls. Then he commissioned them to decorate the ceiling of the loggia; a new and economical method making for a spectacular result. Garnier could thus entrust the vault and floors of the avant-foyer to his mosaicists, an important space because of its size and location. Only the four central panels of the vault designed by Alfred de Curzon—too difficult— were executed in Venice.

**Grand foyer,
west octagonal salon.**
At first, Garnier had planned
to separate the grand foyer
from the two octagonal salons
that extend it to the east and
west by a wall against which
the fireplaces were to stand;
to make the perspective
even more impressive,
he pushed the fireplaces
back to their present location.
Made of sumptuous marble,
they support gilt electroplated
bronze caryatids sculpted
by Charles Cordier
as well as a monumental
Sèvres vase (2 metres high)
by Joseph Chéret.
The paintings are by Félix
Barrias (Prix de Rome, 1844).
The oval ceiling features
The Glorification of Harmony—
that of the planets.
The three tympanums
celebrate rustic, dramatic,
and amorous music.

Right-hand page

**Grand foyer,
east octagonal salon.**
The fireplace caryatids are
by Albert Carrier-Belleuse,
who produced the groups
of torchères of the grand
staircase. As for the vase,
it is blue (it is celadon
in the west).
The paintings in this salon
are by Élie Delaunay
(Prix de Rome, 1856).
Delivered at the eleventh hour
in late 1874, they are very
modern in their technique.
On the ceiling is a zodiac.
The three tympanums feature
Orpheus and Eurydice,
Apollo Receiving the Lyre,
and *Amphion Building Cities
with the Sound of His Lyre*—
a metaphor for the affinity
between music and
architecture; a perfect
subject in this setting.

Imagination
(*Η ΕΙΔΩΛΟΠΟΙΑ*)
by Maximilien Bourgeois.
Plaster gilded with
two types of gold, 1872.
The grand foyer is not
just about painting; many
sculptures contribute
to its splendour.
At the top of each column,
twenty statues personify
the qualities required
by artists; the name of each
of them is inscribed in Greek
on its base. To begin with,
there were supposed
to be twenty-four of them;
over the years, some
of them disappeared (*Work,
Conscience, Study,* and
Power); others—sometimes
unexpected—appeared.
Then the list was reduced
to twenty statues—including
Imagination by Bourgeois—
entrusted to as many artists.

Charles Garnier
by Jean-Baptiste Carpeaux.
Electroplated bronze.
Signed and dated
"Bte Carpeaux 1869".
This masterpiece was
executed by Carpeaux
while he was working on
The Dance. It was described
by Théophile Gautier as
"more alive than life itself";
Ernest Chesnau wrote:
"The model was superb:
small, thin, bony, angular,
fretful, tense… a strange air,
as if primitive, naive,
barbaric, and gentle,
underscored by a blend of
Arab, Florentine, Byzantine,
and the Rue Mouffetard."
Garnier was very proud of it.
This copy was given to
the Opéra by Louise Garnier
in November 1904.
By chance, after restoration,
it encountered a mosaic
by Chagall, which curiously
serves as its backdrop here.

**East octagonal salon,
at the edge of the
grand foyer,** details.
The Palais Garnier swarms
with details, and its forest
hides hundreds of trees.
Here, on the left, one of the
torchères by Félix Chabaud,
Oil, with an ancient lamp
as a hat and olive branches
as a necklace; on the right,
a glimpse of Alfred Darvant's
ornamental sculptures—
ten years of work.
"He understood everything I
wanted. Darvant thinks big;
he works quickly and well,"
wrote Garnier
(*Le Nouvel Opéra*, 136).

**The grand foyer
on a gala evening.**
At the Opéra, as in love,
"too much is not enough"
(*The Marriage of Figaro*,
libretto by Lorenzo da Ponte
set to music by
Wolfgang Amadeus Mozart).

The Salon de la Lune.
In the west salon, the Salon de la Lune, it is white gold, not yellow gold, that streams: silver rays sprinkled with gold constellations, platinum leaf decoration with gold highlights. As in the Salon du Soleil, four mirrors, backed with silver (and not with gold), set up infinite reflections of the light of the chandelier, creating a fantastical atmosphere. As for the central silver and gold discs, they are filled with swirling bats and owls (Salon de la Lune) or crawling salamanders (Salon du Soleil). Garnier was very critical of the final result, which he described as the decoration at the "bottom of a chocolate box lined with foil" (*Le Nouvel Opéra*, 163).

The Salon du Soleil.
The two small circular salons were named the Salon du Soleil and the Salon de la Lune by Garnier. Their themes were hot and cold, as they were supposed to be vestibules: the first for the smoking room, the second for the Galerie du Glacier.

Their decoration, which Garnier considered provisional, was painted in great haste just before the inauguration by the famous decorators Auguste Rubé and Philippe Chaperon; in the rush to finish, the themes were reversed.

"And that is why, if the smoking room were finished, one would go through ice to show that this is the place to light up a cigar, and why one now passes through fire to show that this is the place to have a sorbet," concluded Garnier philosophically (*Le Nouvel Opéra*, 164).

Salon du Glacier.
Unfinished when the building
was inaugurated in 1875,
the salon only took on its
present appearance in 1889.
A few works of art executed
before 1875 had been put
in place, in particular the
Gobelins tapestries (1873–74);
the fresh *Bacchanalia*
of the ceiling was painted
by Georges Clairin in 1889.
Flanking the entrance
are two of the eighty busts
decorating the corridors and
public areas of the Opéra:
the dancer Marie Taglioni by
Laure Martin Coutan (1888)
and the conductor
François Habeneck
by François Captier (1888).

**Salon du Glacier,
near the entrance.**
An architectural ensemble
of rare elegance.
In this photograph, four of
the eight Gobelins tapestries
executed after cartoons
by Alexis Mazerolle;
from left to right, *Hunting*,
Tea, *Coffee*, and *Peaches*.
Four busts of noteworthy
figures in the history of opera:
François Lays
by Henri Allouard,

Rosalie Levasseur
by Henri Vernhes,
Étienne de Jouy
by Adolphe Eude,
and *Mlle Maillard*
by Laure Martin Coutan;
made out of Carrara marble,
they rest on plinths carved
out of the most beautiful
and rarest marbles.
Above the tapestries
are masks by Chabaud:
Io, *Bacchus*, *Venus*,
and *Hercules*.

Tea by Antoine-Ernest Hupé,
1874.
Executed after cartoons
by Alexis-Joseph Mazerolle,
the tapestries of the Salon
du Glacier were woven
by the Gobelins manufactory
between 1873 and 1874.
Designed to hang in pairs
according to their themes,
they are dated and bear the
name of the master weaver
who made them. Originally,
their grounds were blue.
During the interval, like
in all the foyers, the dream
continues: through the magic
of tea, the symbol of all
that is exotic.

In depth

Opera and ballet at the Palais Garnier

When it moved into the Palais Garnier in 1875, the Opéra no longer had any scenery or costumes; they had been destroyed in the fire of 1873. The priority was to recreate a repertoire. At that time, the directors were concessionaires, received a fixed subsidy and operated at their own risk. Consequently, the first director, Olivier Halanzier, revived the successes of the Salle Le Peletier: Halévy's *La Juive*, Meyerbeer's *Les Huguenots*, Donizetti's *La favorite*, Rossini's evergreen *William Tell*, and two recent triumphs, Ambroise Thomas' *Hamlet* and Gounod's *Faust*. As for the ballet, its presence was obligatory in all operas at the time, even if it meant inventing choreography—which is what happened when Mozart's *Don Giovanni* was revived in 1875. Halanzier also put on Léo Delibes' *Coppélia* from 1875 and produced *Sylvia*, also by Delibes, for the first time in 1876.

In 1879 Halanzier was replaced by Auguste Vaucorbeil, who succeeded in inviting Giuseppe Verdi to direct *Aida* in 1880, but who died in harness in 1884. Then a singer, Pedro Gailhard, took over the reins for many years. Alone or in partnership, he energetically ran the theatre until 1908 (except in 1892–93). Although he still favoured the "grand opera" so loved by the public, he also developed the Verdian (*Rigoletto* in 1885, *Otello* in 1894) and Wagnerian repertoires. In 1891 *Lohengrin* sparked a riot outside and a triumph inside the theatre; then came *Die Walküre*, a reprise of *Tannhäuser* (staged

at Salle Le Peletier in 1861, a tremendous scandal, even then), *Die Meistersinger von Nürnberg*, *Siegfried*, and *Tristan und Isolde*. This period ended in an event, the first concert of Russian music with Fyodor Chaliapine organised by Sergei Diaghilev, a prelude to the splendours of the "Saisons russes", then of the "Ballets Russes". Gailhard showed little interest in ballet, though. His directorship was also marked by a few initiatives that lived on: matinee performances, the inscription of the conductor's name on the bill, and the fixing of the conductor's position in the orchestra pit. There was another tragedy during his rule: in 1894 the scenery room of the Opéra went up in flames. Everything had to be remade.

In 1908 a duo took over the reins: composer André Messager and manager Leimistin Broussan. Despite their disagreements, they introduced a new repertoire: 18th-century French operas (Jean-Philippe Rameau's *Hippolyte et Aricie*), first productions (Richard Strauss's *Salome*), further works by Wagner (*Götterdämmerung*, *Das Rheingold*, *Parsifal*; several complete cycles of *Der Ring des Nibelungen* between 1911 and 1913), and invitations to foreign companies (in 1908, within the context of Diaghilev's "Saisons russes", the Moscow Imperial Theatre gave a legendary performance of Modest Mussorgsky's *Boris Godunov* with Chaliapine). From 1910, Diaghilev's company, henceforth devoted to dance, gave dazzling annual performances that revived the house ballet.

Maria Callas in Vincenzo Bellini's *Norma*.
After her sensational departure from Rome, Maria Callas moved to Paris, where she died on 16 September 1977, aged fifty-three.
Her first appearance on stage at the Palais Garnier, in December 1958, is engraved in the memories of those present, as were her iconic interpretations of the roles of Tosca and Norma.

In 1914 an exceptional personality was appointed director: Jacques Rouché. A graduate of the École Polytechnique, he had a passion for theatre and had successfully run the Théâtre des Arts, where music had an important place. He remained at the helm for thirty years and was the last director-entrepreneur, as well as the greatest. Under Rouché, first productions and revivals followed one another: a new spectacle every fortnight on average. Major works became part of the repertoire: Hector Berlioz's *Les Troyens*, Verdi's *La Traviata* and *Falstaff*, *Don Giovanni*—at last—in the original language and Mozart's *Die Zauberflöte*, Mussorgsky's *Khovanshchina*, Giacomo Puccini's *Tosca* and *Turandot*, Richard Strauss's *Der Rosenkavalier* and

Elektra, Gioachino Rossini's *L'Italiana in Algeri*, Vincenzo Bellini's *Norma*, and *Der fliegende Holländer*, the only major Wagnerian opera that had not yet been presented at the Opéra de Paris. And ballet was not left out in the cold: the Ballets Russes returned in 1919 and the "house" productions opened one after the other, spurred on by Albert Aveline, then, from 1938, by Serge Lifar; the first *défilé du corps de ballet* took place in 1926.

Even before the Second World War, the French state played a growing role in the management of the Opéra and the Opéra-Comique in the framework of the Réunion des Théâtres Lyriques Nationaux. Officials came and went, the management was made up of civil servants, and the situation gradually got worse, despite the efforts of a few talented men. Georges Hirsh, general administrator from 1947 to 1951, then from 1956 to 1959, produced for the first time Darius Milhaud's *Bolivar*, Verdi's *Un ballo in maschera*, and Francis Poulenc's *Dialogues des Carmélites*, and, in 1958, invited Maria Callas for a legendary concert. Maurice Lehmann, general administrator from 1951 to 1955, in 1952 revived Rameau's *Les Indes galantes* in an outstanding production and staged Weber's *Oberon* for the first time. Gabriel Dussurget, founder of the

Festival d'Aix-en-Provence, artistic adviser to the Opéra from 1959 to 1969, confided to Raymond Rouleau the staging of an unforgettable *Carmen* by Georges Bizet with sets by Lila de Nobili.

Under the directorship of Georges Auric from 1962 to 1968, the situation became worrying despite a few high notes (the premiere of Alban Berg's *Wozzeck*, brilliant productions of Verdi's *Don Carlos*, *Norma* with Maria Callas, and Puccini's *Turandot* with Birgit Nilsson). Jacques Duhamel, minister of culture, then called on the Swiss composer Rolf

Liebermann, who masterfully directed the Hamburgerische Staatsoper. With his arrival in Paris in 1973, the Opéra de Paris became a permanent international festival. Liebermann regenerated the chorus and orchestra, and replaced the system of alternating performances with that of a series of performances of the same work, which enabled productions to become more polished and the best performers to be engaged. From *Le nozze di Figaro*, staged by Giorgio Strehler and directed by Sir Georg Solti in 1973, to the world premiere

of Alban Berg's *Lulu* completed by Friedrich Cerha and staged by Patrice Chéreau in 1979, the Liebermann seasons delighted audiences. In 1980 Liebermann left the Opéra de Paris, which thanks to him had become one of the most prestigious in the world.

The construction of the Opéra Bastille and uncertainty about the future weighed heavily on the four directors who came after Liebermann in quick succession until 13 July 1989, the date of the inauguration of the new theatre. After a few years of the Palais Garnier being exclusively used for ballet while the Opéra Bastille was devoted to opera, the two venues introduced an enlightened policy of role-sharing after the appointment of Hugues Gall as director of both in 1995. Since then, the venues for operas and ballets have been chosen according to their nature and scale: lavish performances at Bastille, more intimate operas (about fifty performances a year) and the majority of ballets (a hundred or so performances by one of the best companies in the world) at the Palais Garnier. This system of sharing was continued by Gall's successors, Gérard Mortier (2004–9) and Nicolas Joël.

Hugues Gall also received approval from the Centre des Monuments Nationaux for an ambitious restoration plan for the building, which concerned the stage house and the auditorium (1995–96), the façade (2000), and the foyers (2003–4).

Rudolf Nureyev and Yvette Chauviré in *Giselle*, 1962. The greatest dancer of his generation requested asylum in Paris on 17 June 1961. He often returned to the city to dance with the greatest partners, directed the Ballet de l'Opéra from 1983 to 1989, and remained the principal choreographer. He, too, died in France, on 6 January 1993; he was fifty-five years old and had been dancing a few months earlier, on 8 October 1992, during the first production of his version of *La Bayadère* with music by Léon Minkus at the Opéra.

The Phantom of the Opera

One evening, the famous Italian prima donna Carlotta was singing her finest role, Marguerite in *Faust* (opera in five acts by Jules Barbier and Michel Carré, music by Charles Gounod), at the Palais Garnier; her partners included the tenor Carolus Fonta in the title role and Christine Daaé in that of Siébel. The theatre was packed, filled mainly with admirers of the beautiful Carlotta. The two associate directors of the Opéra, Moncharmin and Richard, were in their box, box no. 5 of the dress circle, the one just behind the proscenium, on the Head of State Pavilion side. One of them noticed, in the middle of the stalls, a fat, rather vulgar woman dressed in black, flanked by two coarse-looking men, and asked the other who "those" were. His associate explained that he had invited his concierge, her brother, and her husband, who had never been to the opera.

During the third act, La Carlotta triumphantly sang the king of Thule aria and was cheered at the end of the jewel aria. Encouraged by this success, she gave her all in the following duet, in which Faust, on his knees, implores her: "Let me gaze at your face." She replied: "I'm listening! . . . And I understand that lonely voice singing in my heart!"

At that moment, a terrible, extraordinary thing happened. The audience stood up all at once and the two directors could not hold back an exclamation of horror. Carlotta herself was speechless: from her mouth had escaped an obscene creature, a toad—

a "co-ack", a horrifying "co-ack"! In the auditorium, the astonishment was followed by confusion; dumbfounded, the audience shared their consternation. On the stage, Fonta looked at Carlotta with an incredible expression of childlike astonishment, while the alarmed faces of a few extras could be seen in the wings.

In box no. 5, the two directors were trembling at the thought that the worst was yet to come. However, after a few seconds, Richard pulled himself together and shouted at Carlotta: "Well, go on!" Bravely, Carlotta started afresh on the fatal line at the end of which the toad had appeared. And the toad also started afresh: "CO-ACK!"

There was an uproar in the auditorium. Then the stunned directors heard a voice that came from somewhere unknown whisper in their right ears: "She is singing tonight to bring the chandelier down!" They barely had time to raise their eyes to look at it before the immense bronze and crystal chandelier of the Palais Garnier plunged from the ceiling and came crashing down amidst shouts of terror and a wild rush for the doors.

There were several injured and one death. The following day, a newspaper appeared with this headline, which was not in the best of taste: "Two hundred kilos on the head of a concierge!" It exaggerated the weight a little.

The reader will have certainly recognised in this summary one of the most famous passages of Maurice Leroux's novel, *Le Fantôme de l'Opéra*. And so, this was a true story—well, almost. In fact, Gaston Leroux drew his inspiration from two historical incidents, only one of which took place at the Palais Garnier. The other happened in London in 1791. That evening was the premier of the great composer Franz Joseph Haydn's Symphony No. 96 in D major. It was the fourth symphony whose premiere Haydn had successfully conducted himself: from the beginning, London audiences loved it. At the end of the final movement, which was

Red Death, in Rupert Julian's film *The Phantom of the Opera* (1925). Red Death is, of course, Erik the phantom, brilliantly played by Lon Chaney. And Satan calls the turns, both on the grand staircase and on the stage, where Gounod's *Faust* is being performed.

The bronze and crystal chandelier of the Opéra. Garnier spent a long time designing it before it was modelled by Corboz. It comprises 340 lights and weighs 7 tonnes. It was made by the firm Lacarrière, Delatour et Cie and cost 30,000 gold francs (275,000 euros).

encored, the enthusiastic spectators rushed at the composer, who was seated at the harpsichord as was the custom at the time, and thus deserted the centre of the stalls. At that moment, the large auditorium chandelier fell from the ceiling and crashed onto the floor. No one was hurt as the stalls had just been emptied. After the initial terror had subsided, the audience shouted, "Miracle!" This word became the name of the symphony.

Sadly, there was no such miracle at the Palais Garnier. On 20 May 1896, a forgotten work by an equally forgotten composer, *Helle* by Alphonse Duvernoy, was being performed. The annual *Les Annales du théâtre et de la musique* said: "It was exactly three minutes to nine. The first act was drawing to a close. Madame Caron's song had just been encored when a tremendous noise was heard. At the same time, a bright light appeared, as quick as lightning, followed by a cloud of dust that rose from the top of the auditorium to the rigging loft. We first thought it was an explosion or an anarchist attack. The audience rushed towards the exits. But with admirable sangfroid, Delmas, Madame Caron, and the members of the chorus who were on stage stayed put in the hope that their composure would reassure the audience. They succeeded in reassuring the spectators on the ground floor and the first two levels. But upstairs, in the gallery where the supposed explosion had taken

place, there was considerable panic. People were jostling each other, and female members of the audience attempted to get over the railing to jump into the auditorium. The guards stopped them from doing so and led them to the exit. Thanks to them, there were no incidents."

Initially, only a few injuries were recorded—mostly contusions. "We began to hope that the accident would not have serious consequences when screams attracted the attention of one of the municipal guards. He retraced his steps and found a woman trapped under a girder; her leg and right eye had been injured by the fallen girder underneath which she was stuck. At the same time, a girl, her face bloody, began to call for her mother who, she said, was under the rubble. There was a search and, in an excavation hollowed out in the gallery floor and covered by cast-iron blocks, the horribly mutilated body of a middle-aged woman was discovered. It was the woman the girl was looking for: Madame Chomette, aged fifty-six, concierge."

Then the cause of accident began to be understood: "We realised when we were removing the body of Madame Chomette from the rubble," continued the

annual. "[The accident] had been caused by the fall of one of the chandelier counterweights. The large central chandelier of the theatre is supported by eight iron-wire ropes as thick as a wrist, each of which has a counterweight weighing about 700 kilograms on the end of it. Each counterweight is this heavy so that in case one or more ropes breaks, the chandelier is still supported. Along the length of one of these wires, slipped into a sort of recess, called a 'chimney' in the language of the theatre, was a cable used for electric lighting. Wear produced a contact, the electric cable ignited, and the intense spark produced melted the wire supporting the counterweight. The enormous mass fell down the 'chimney', smashed through first the ceiling, then the floor of the fifth gallery in a spot where fortunately no one was seated, crushed seats 11 and 13 of the fourth gallery occupied by Madame Chomette

and her daughter, and then demolished the wooden floor underneath them before going out."

Seats 11 and 13 of the fourth gallery still exist—in the first row opposite the stage, they are excellent seats. An interesting detail: the chandelier counterweights have been removed.

The water tank located underneath the Opéra stage, 19th-century photograph published in *L'Illustration*. The real truth of the "lake" protecting the dwelling place of Erik, the love-crazy phantom. Usually filled with water, the tanks are drained every ten years and accessible through two manholes.

The entrance of the "house on the lake". The poetic truth. In the silent film *The Phantom of the Opera* (1925), it is in this bewitched house surrounded by water that Erik the phantom (Lon Chaney) hides the singer Christine (Mary Philbin) after having abducted her in mid-performance right under the noses of dumbfounded Parisians.

Centre des monuments nationaux
President
Isabelle Lemesle
Managing director
Pierre Deprost

Publishing director
Dominique Seridji
Publications coordinator
Denis Picard
Assistant publications coordinator
Karin Franques

Editorial and documentation coordinator
Anne-Sophie Grouhel - Le Tellec
Translator
Chrisoula Petridis
Copy editor
Susan Schneider
Graphic design
Régis Dutreuil
Layout
Sylvie Lelandais
Production coordinator
Carine Merse

Photoengraving
MCP, Saran
Printing
Mame, Tours, France

Abbreviations
BMO: Bibliothèque-Musée de l'Opéra;
BNF: Bibliothèque Nationale de France;
CMN: Centre des Monuments Nationaux.

Photographic credits
All photographs by Jean-Pierre Delagarde except Akg-images/album:
61, 63b; Ullstein Bild/Roger-Viollet: 60; BNF: 8, 12b; *L'Illustration*/
Keystone: 63t; RMN/Gérard Blot: 4; RMN (Musée d'Orsay)/
Hervé Lewandowski: 14; © Studio Lipnitzki/Roger-Viollet: 59.
© ADAGP, Paris, for the work of Marc Chagall: 13, 42, 53r, 62.

© Éditions du patrimoine
Centre des monuments nationaux
Paris, 2010
Dépôt légal: June 2010   ISBN: 978-2-7577-0095-2

Acknowledgements
I would first of all like to pay homage to Hugues Gall, member
of the Académie des Beaux-Arts and former director of the Opéra
de Paris, who initiated the recent restoration programmes
at the Palais Garnier and to whom this book owes so much.

My sincere thanks go to Nicolas Joel, director of the Opéra National
de Paris, and to Christophe Ghristi, the Opéra's stagecraft director,
who made this new publication on the Palais Garnier possible.

Thanks are also due to Jean-Yves Kaced, Stéphane Löber,
and Gilles Djeraouane of the Opéra de Paris, Alexandre Antoine
of the Galerie de l'Opéra de Paris, and Mathias Auclair
of the Bibliothèque-Musée de l'Opéra de Paris for their assistance
and advice. I was delighted to be able to work once more with
Éditions du patrimoine and its team, particularly Anne-Sophie
Grouhel - Le Tellec and Jean-Pierre Delagarde.

Illustrations, cover, and opening pages
Front cover: The main façade of the Palais Garnier at night.
Page 15: *Lyric Drama* by Joseph Perraud, detail. Échaillon limestone.
On the left of Perraud's group, a naked man, armed with
a gladiator's sword, his foot on the traitor's outstretched arm,
tears off the drapery covering the latter. Garnier commented:
"Perraud, with his somewhat fierce and unsociable nature, with his
instinct of independence, found it difficult to submit to the demands
of architectural decoration; it should be acknowledged that,
among the figures of the sculpture, the corpse and the man removing
the shroud are exceptionally well executed. Of all the groups
of the Opéra, it is perhaps these pieces that are most powerful
and the best studies of muscles" (*Le Nouvel Opéra*, 429).
Page 58: *Apollo, Poetry, and Music* by Aimé Millet, 1869.
Partially gilt bronze by Denière.
As Garnier said, this proud silhouette is the "sign" of the monument.
This is quite natural as Apollo was the god of music.
As a mark of the sovereignty of Apollo, the god is found everywhere,
often represented by his instrument. Garnier strewed the building
with lyres, declaring himself "guilty with premeditation. Owing to
a consensus of opinion, the lyre represents music: it would probably
be more innovative to use another instrument, but I imagine that it
will be some time before artists replace the convention with a grand
piano or a hurdy-gurdy" (*Le Nouvel Opéra*, 65). He described
the proliferation of lyres as an "act of archaeological foresight":
as a consequence, it would be easier to identify the future ruins.